A Home for Henrietta

Written by Helen Docherty

Illustrated by Felicia Whaley

Callum found the woodlouse taking shelter under a stone in his back garden.

"What are you doing under there?" asked Callum. "You could've got squashed."

He picked her up, very gently. Her tiny feet tickled his hand.

Callum knew then that her name was Henrietta, and that he was going to give her a home.

2

He carried Henrietta to the old dolls' house and tipped her carefully inside.

"This is your new home, Henrietta!" said Callum.

"Who's Henrietta?"

Callum's big sister, Summer, was peering over his shoulder.

3

"A woodlouse!" laughed Summer.
"She looks a bit funny in there."

They both looked at Henrietta. Her
feet were skidding on the shiny floor.

"I don't think a dolls' house is the right habitat for a woodlouse," said Summer. "The floor is too slippery, and there's no source of food for her in there."

Callum thought for a moment.

"I know!" he said.

Callum found an old shoebox and filled it with grass and twigs from the garden.

Then he raced back to Henrietta.

Summer was reading from a book about bugs:

"Woodlice are simple organisms. They look like insects, but actually they are animals with a hard shell, like crabs."

Callum scooped Henrietta into his palm. Her shell shone like armour. She wasn't simple. She was perfect!

He slid her into the shoebox.

"This will be a better home for you, Henrietta!"

Henrietta scuttled around inside the box.

Callum wondered if
Henrietta was hungry.

"Let's see what woodlice eat," said Summer. "Look, here's a picture of a garden food chain. The plants are producers — they make food — and woodlice are consumers, because they eat the plants."

"Which plants?" asked Callum.

"Rotten ones," said Summer.

Callum ran to the food waste bin and picked out an old apple core.

"Here you are, Henrietta!"

But Henrietta ignored the apple core.

"Let's take the box outside," suggested Summer, "and put some rotten leaves in it."

Henrietta seemed more interested in the leaves.

Callum smiled, and lay down in the grass.

9

Suddenly, a dark shadow swooped down towards the box: a bird!

Callum jumped up and waved his arms wildly to scare it away.

"Do birds eat woodlice?" he asked.

"Their main predators are shrews, toads and spiders," read Summer. "Woodlice are also prey to birds. Henrietta, you had a lucky escape!"

Callum grabbed the box. He needed to find somewhere safe for Henrietta, away from the threat of being eaten …

... somewhere like the garden shed.

No birds could get Henrietta in here!

It was very hot inside the shed. Callum started to feel thirsty. He looked at Henrietta.

"Do you think she's getting too hot?" he asked.

Summer skimmed the page. "Woodlice depend on moisture to survive. They shelter from the sun under rocks or stones, where it's damp."

Callum quickly carried Henrietta's box back outside.

He sat down to think.

He had wanted to give Henrietta a home, but maybe she didn't want to live in a house or a shed — or a box. Maybe the best home for her was in the garden.

"It says here that woodlice break down leaves, which adds goodness to the soil, so things can grow," said Summer. "They help to create a healthy garden environment."

She smiled at Callum. "Henrietta's got a really important job!"

Callum nodded. He knew it was the right thing to do, but it wasn't easy.

Very carefully, he placed Henrietta back under her stone, where she belonged.

"Good luck, Henrietta!" he whispered.

Published by Pearson Education Limited, 80 Strand, London, WC2R 0RL.

www.pearsonschools.co.uk

Text © Pearson Education Limited 2020

Written by Helen Docherty

Project managed and edited by Just Content Limited

Original illustrations © Pearson Education Limited 2020

Illustrated by Felicia Whaley

Designed and typeset by Collaborate Agency Limited

First published 2020

23 22 21 20

10 9 8 7 6 5 4 3 2 1

British Library Cataloguing in Publication Data

A catalogue record for this book is available from the British Library

ISBN 978 0 435 20167 8

Printed in Slovakia by Neografia

Note from the publisher

Pearson has robust editorial processes, including answer and fact checks, to ensure the accuracy of the content in this publication, and every effort is made to ensure this publication is free of errors. We are, however, only human, and occasionally errors do occur. Pearson is not liable for any misunderstandings that arise as a result of errors in this publication, but it is our priority to ensure that the content is accurate. If you spot an error, please do contact us at resourcescorrections@pearson.com so we can make sure it is corrected.